Meet a Baby Moose

Tamika M. Murray

Lerner Publications ◆ Minneapolis

For the Moose

Lerner Publications Company
An imprint of Lerner Publishing Group, Inc.
241 First Avenue North
Minneapolis, MN 55401 USA

For reading levels and more information, look up this title at www.lernerbooks.com.

Main body text set in Billy Infant Regular. Typeface provided by SparkType.

Map illustration on page 20 by Laura K. Westlund.

Library of Congress Cataloging-in-Publication Data

Names: Murray, Tamika M., author.
Title: Meet a baby moose / Tamika M. Murray.
Description: Minneapolis, MN : Lerner Publications, [2024] | Series: Lightning bolt books. Baby North American animals | Includes bibliographical references and index. | Audience: Ages 6-9 | Audience: Grades 2-3 | Summary: "Discover the life of a baby moose! Learn all about these cute animals and what their young life is like, including what they eat, how big they grow, and more"— Provided by publisher.
Identifiers: LCCN 2022037605 (print) | LCCN 2022037606 (ebook) | ISBN 9781728491134 (lib. bdg.) | ISBN 9781728498386 (eb pdf)
Subjects: LCSH: Moose—Infancy—North America—Juvenile literature.
Classification: LCC QL737.U55 M868 2024 (print) | LCC QL737.U55 (ebook) | DDC 599.65/71392—dc23/eng/20220809

LC record available at https://lccn.loc.gov/2022037605
LC ebook record available at https://lccn.loc.gov/2022037606

Manufactured in the United States of America
1-53044-51062-10/20/2022

Table of Contents

Birth of a Baby Moose

A baby moose, or calf, is born in the forest. It grew inside its mom for eight months. A newborn calf weighs 25 to 35 pounds (11 to 16 kg), or a little more than a car tire.

Calves can walk within a few hours after birth. All moose have poor eyesight. But they have a strong sense of hearing and smell at birth.

A calf walks in a field.

A cow with two calves

An adult female moose is called a cow. Cows give birth to one or two calves each mating season. They give birth in late May to early June.

Moose Calf and Mom

Cows protect their calves. Male moose, or bulls, do not help raise the calves.

A calf lying with its mom

A calf spends most of its time with its mom. The calf will go with its mom as she searches for food.

The main predators of moose are black bears, grizzly bears, humans, and wolves. Cows will go after a predator to keep their young safe.

Moose will go after predators like wolves.

A young moose

Calves grow fast. They can gain about 2.2 pounds (1 kg) a day the first five months.

When they grow up, they will be even bigger. Bulls often weigh 794 to 1,323 pounds (360 to 600 kg). Cows often weigh 595 to 882 pounds (270 to 400 kg). But some grow even bigger.

Many calves will grow at least as big as their mom.

Milk and Plants

Cows nurse their calves for about five months. Then calves are weaned.

A moose
eating plants

Calves start to eat plants
at three weeks old. Moose
are herbivores and eat only
plants. Adults and calves eat
a lot of water plants. Water
plants help moose be strong.

Moose spend lots of time in or near water. Water helps moose stay cool in the summer.

A calf and cow cool down in water.

Moose often eat while standing in water.

Water also protects moose. Standing in water makes it hard for other animals to attack.

Growing Up

A calf and its mom stay together for about one year. The mom makes the calf leave before she has another calf. The calf lives alone after leaving its mom.

A bull next to a cow

Moose start to mate around two years old. They have calves once every one to two years. But they are not fully grown until they are four or five years old.

Moose live for ten to twelve years in the wild. Their first year of life can be dangerous due to predators and other threats.

A full-grown moose

Moose spend their time eating, swimming, and traveling. Their calves help the life cycle continue!

Moose Life Cycle

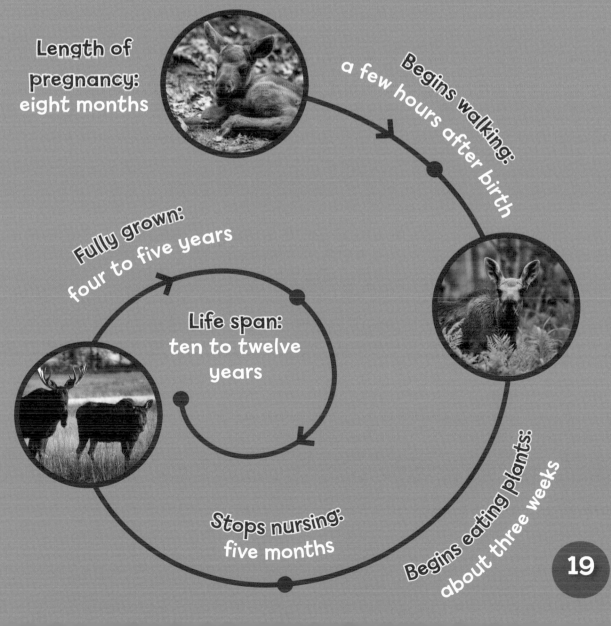

Length of pregnancy: eight months

Begins walking: a few hours after birth

Fully grown: four to five years

Life span: ten to twelve years

Stops nursing: five months

Begins eating plants: about three weeks

Habitat in Focus

- In North America, moose live in Canada, the northern United States, and the Rocky Mountains.

- Moose live in forests.

- Moose can't sweat and usually stay in cool areas.

Fun Facts

- Bulls grow new antlers every spring. The antlers fall off in the early winter.

- Moose eat 30 to 40 pounds (14 to 18 kg) of food each day during the summer and as many twigs as they can find in winter.

- Moose are related to deer.

- Adult moose can run up to 35 miles (56 km) per hour.

- Moose may experience heat stress in temperatures above 57°F (14°C) in summer and 23°F (-5°C) in winter.

Glossary

forest: a large area of trees and bushes where moose live

herbivore: an animal that eats plants

life cycle: the different stages an animal such as a moose goes through during its life

mating season: the period of the year when moose mate and have calves

nurse: when a baby drinks milk from its mom

predator: an animal that preys on other animals

water plant: a plant that grows and lives in water instead of on land

wean: when an animal no longer relies on milk from nursing to survive

Learn More

Boothroyd, Jennifer. *Baby Moose*. Minneapolis: Bearport, 2022.

Britannica Kids: Moose
https://kids.britannica.com/kids/article/moose/384796

Chang, Kirsten. *Moose or Elk?* Minneapolis: Bellwether Media, 2021.

Moose
https://www.maine.gov/sos/kids/about/wildlife/moose

Moose—Where and How They Live
https://easyscienceforkids.com/all-about-moose/

Murray, Tamika M. *Meet a Baby Gray Wolf*. Minneapolis: Lerner Publications, 2024.

Index

Photo Acknowledgments

Image credits: Holger Ehlers Naturephoto/Alamy Stock Photo, pp. 4, 19; NEIL SMITH/Alamy Stock Photo, p. 5; Ray Bulson/Alamy Stock Photo, p. 6; SBTheGreenMan/Getty Images, p. 7; Niebrugge Images/Alamy Stock Photo, p. 8; Design Pics Inc/Alamy Stock Photo, pp. 9, 14; Cavan Images/Getty Images, p. 10; Chase Dekker Wild-Life Images/Getty Images, pp. 11, 18; Jill Ann Spaulding/Getty Images, p. 12; pchoui/Getty Images, pp. 13, 19; Edwin Remsberg/Getty Images, p. 15; Heather Stewman/Getty Images, p. 16; Mark Newman/Getty Images, pp. 17, 19.

Cover: mlharing/Getty Images.